# Old-Time Quilting Designs

SHIRLEY THOMPSON

**POWELL**
PUBLICATIONS
P.O. BOX 513 ■ EDMONDS, WA 98020

**Dedicated to Tracy, John, Rick, Martina and Anneke Nicole.**

# INTRODUCTION

OLD-TIME QUILTING DESIGNS contains over ninety full-size traditional designs that were popular from the late 1800's through the 1930's, as well as several original designs. The designs for blocks, borders and lattice strips range from one-inch to eighteen-inches in size. Quilting fundamentals are introduced along with equipment needed. Also included are directions for marking, basting and quilting.

# QUILTING

A quilt consists of three layers: top, batting and backing. Quilting stitches hold the three layers together while adding ornamental surface interest to the quilt.

The actual quilting stitch is a simple running stitch. It is more important to have stitches of equal length and spacing than to have tiny uneven stitches. The stitches on the back should be the same size as those on the top.

Some quiltmakers push the needle up and down with the end of a thimble on the sewing hand, and using a rocking motion, make a quick succession of stitches. Others hold the eye of the needle between the thumb and index finger, and after taking several small stitches, use the thimble to push through all three layers of the quilt. A stenographer's rubber file finger is helpful in preventing the eye of the needle from biting into the tip of the forefinger, and aids in pulling the needle through the quilt.

To begin quilting, knot an eighteen-inch length of quilting thread and pull it from the top into the batting a short distance from where you plan to start. Tug lightly on the thread to pop the knot into the batting. If the knot resists going through the top, it may be necessary to enlarge the opening with your needle. To end the quilting, tie a knot a short distance from your needle. Make a final stitch through the top and batting. Pull the knot through to the inside of the batting a needle length or two away, bring it up through the top and cut the threads. For a look of perfection, it should be impossible to tell where the quilting line begins and ends.

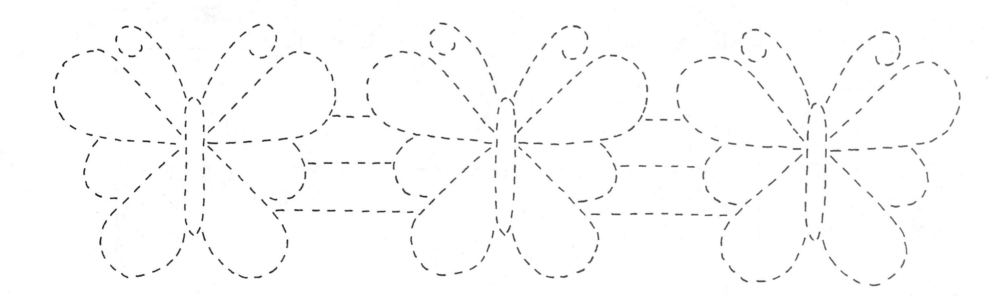

Although the average person is struck first by color and design, upon closer inspection it becomes obvious that much of a quilt's beauty is in the quilting itself. Our great-grandmothers considered fine stitchery as important as the piecing, and today, fine quilting and intricate designs greatly increase the value of old quilts to collectors.

The quilting pattern is an important part of the overall design and care must be taken in choosing a design that compliments the pieced or appliqued top. For appliqued or fancy pieced tops, a simple outline or overall quilting design is most often used. For a plain top, or top with alternating plain blocks, a more complex design is appropriate.

Outline stitching is the most common form of quilting. To outline, follow the shape of each piece in the pattern about one-fourth inch from the seam line within each shape.

Contour, or echo stitching, is quilting with lines one-fourth to one-half inch apart following the lines of the pattern until the space is filled.

Filler quilting patterns add contrast and surface interest to the more elaborate designs in borders and open areas.

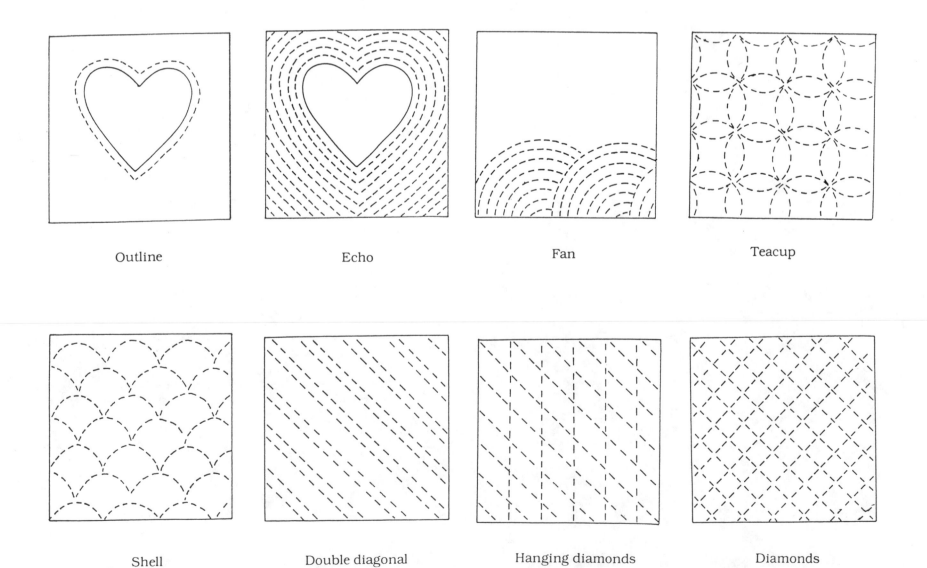

| Outline | Echo | Fan | Teacup |

| Shell | Double diagonal | Hanging diamonds | Diamonds |

# EQUIPMENT

## THIMBLE

The thimble is a necessary tool in quilting and is worn on the middle finger of the sewing hand. Choose a thimble with deep indentations on the sides and top to prevent your needle from slipping. Many quilters wear a leather thimble on the forefinger of the hand under the quilt.

## THREAD

Quilting thread is best for quilting. It is a strong cotton thread manufactured with a finish to strengthen it and prevent it from knotting. Many colors have become available in the last few years. Using a thread lighter or darker than the background fabric will accent the quilting. If you have not mastered small, even stitches, it would be better to use thread the same color as the background.

## NEEDLES

Quilting needles, often called "betweens," are generally preferred for quilting. A between is a short strong needle that does not bend easily. Size 9 or 10 is most often used and many quilters find that by using a smaller sized needle it is possible to obtain smaller stitches. Quilting needles become smaller as the number increases, with size 12 being the smallest.

## MARKING TOOLS

One of the favorite marking tools today is a blue, felt tipped pen that is "water soluble." The marking lines are removed by completely submerging the quilt in a washer filled with cold water, then running it through the spin cycle. Lay flat to dry. Never wash your quilt with a detergent without first removing the blue lines as it could set the blue into permanent brown lines. If a lead pencil is preferred, a number 3 or 4 semi-hard pencil will give a thin marking line and will not smudge like a soft pencil. Care should be taken to mark lightly because of the difficulty of removing a darker line.

## BATTING

Today most quilters use a bonded polyester batt. It is readily available, lightweight, holds its shape, and has a good loft. It also has a glaze that prevents the fibers from penetrating the top of the quilt and does not require close quilting. Polyester batting is now available in a very light weight which is easy to quilt and gives a look similar to cotton.

Batting made of 100 percent cotton has been the traditional filler for quilts, but it is not a popular choice with today's quiltmakers because of its tendency to lump when washed, if not closely quilted. You can, however, get the look of 100 percent cotton by using a thin glazed batt made of 80 percent cotton and 20 percent polyester. This batt is an excellent choice if you are quilting an old quilt top or simply want to give your quilt an old fashioned look.

## QUILT FRAME

Most experienced quiltmakers prefer a quilting frame. A narrow frame with a ratchet for rolling is a practical choice because it is not too large to leave up until the quilting is completed. Frames also come in a small card table size.

Quilting can also be successfully accomplished on a large 16 to 23 inch quilting hoop. Its size and portability make it popular with those who lack space for a frame. An added advantage is the ability to rotate the hoop allowing you to always quilt toward yourself.

# BACKING

The backing is the bottom layer of the quilt and should be three to four inches larger on all four sides than the top. Choose a fabric that corresponds in color and weight to the top. If backing is to be pieced, place the full width of fabric, with selvages removed, down the center and add an equal amount of fabric to each side.

When using different colors of quilting thread on your project, use printed fabric for the backing, being careful that the print will not show through any light colored fabric on your quilt top. If you plan to use an elaborate quilting design and want the quilting to show on the back as well as the front, do not use a print fabric as it will tend to hide the quilting.

# MARKING

Marking can be accomplished in a number of ways. A stencil can be made by pasting the design on cardboard and cutting narrow slits along the design with an X-acto blade. The electric hot pen is an excellent tool for making plastic stencils. Trace the design directly on stencil plastic with a fine point permanent felt tip marker and cut slits along the design with the electric hot pen. Mark in the slits with your favorite marking tool. Templates can be made for simple designs such as hearts, leaves, and flowers by cutting around the outside edge of the design. Place the template on the quilt top and trace around the design.

Perforated patterns are made by tracing a design on heavy paper and punching holes along the lines of the design with a large darning needle or an unthreaded sewing machine. Position the pattern on the quilt top and rub cornstarch through the holes to mark dark fabric. Use cinnamon to mark light fabric. Carefully remove the pattern and lightly pencil in the design.

A light table provides the easiest and fastest method of marking a quilt top. It is a simple matter to make a light table if you do not have one. Remove the leaves from a kitchen or dining room table. Open the table and place a heavy piece of plate glass over the opening. Tape the outer edges of the glass so that you do not mar the table top. The glass should be at least three inches wider than the table opening. I use a piece of plate glass twenty-eight inches by twenty-four inches and open the table to a width of twenty inches and place the glass lengthwise across the opening. This leaves four inches of glass on each side of the table so that there is no danger of the glass falling through. Place a table lamp with a one hundred watt bulb on the floor beneath the glass. Trace your quilting design on white paper with a medium point felt tip marker and tape it to the glass. Place your quilt top over the lighted glass and trace the design on the quilt. This method is very successful with white and most light to medium colored fabrics. If you are marking the design on black, brown, or navy fabric, trace the quilting pattern on white paper, glue it to heavy brown wrapping paper or black construction paper and punch holes along the design with a large darning needle. Again, place your quilt top over the lighted glass. The light will shine through the holes and enable you to mark your design with a white art pencil.

Masking tape can be used as a quilting guide when quilting straight or diagonal lines. Place a strip of tape where a straight line is to be quilted and quilt along its edge. When the line is quilted, lift the tape and move it to the next area to be quilted. The same piece of tape can be used several times before being discarded. Masking tape comes in a variety of widths including a ¼-inch width which is perfect for outline quilting.

# BASTING

Before basting the three layers of your quilt together, iron the top and backing. Remove the batting from its package, fold it in fourths and allow it to rest overnight so that it will lie flat when you are ready to use it. Lay the backing right-side-down on the floor or other large surface. Place the batting on the backing, smoothing out any wrinkles. Place the top right-side-up on the batting. If your floor is carpeted, pin the backing, batting and top to the carpet with straight pins as each is placed on the floor to hold each layer taut for basting. Baste the three layers together with diagonal lines radiating out from the center. Next, baste in a large grid approximately eight to ten inches apart. Finally, baste around the outer edge.

To put the quilt into the frame, remove the bars from a rolling ratchet type frame and place one bar at the top and one at the bottom of the quilt. Baste the edges of the quilt to the muslin strip on the bars with heavy thread. Have one person hold one bar steady while one or two people begin rolling the quilt on the other bar until it reaches the center of the quilt. Roll the opposite bar to the center and adjust the bars in the frame. Start quilting in the center of the quilt and quilt to the edge of the first half. Re-roll the quilt to the center and quilt to the opposite edge.

Quilting can also be done in a large 23-inch round quilting hoop. Begin quilting in the center of the quilt and quilt out toward the edges.

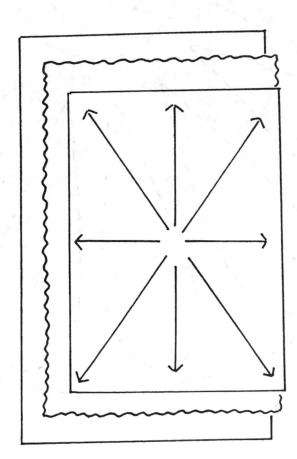

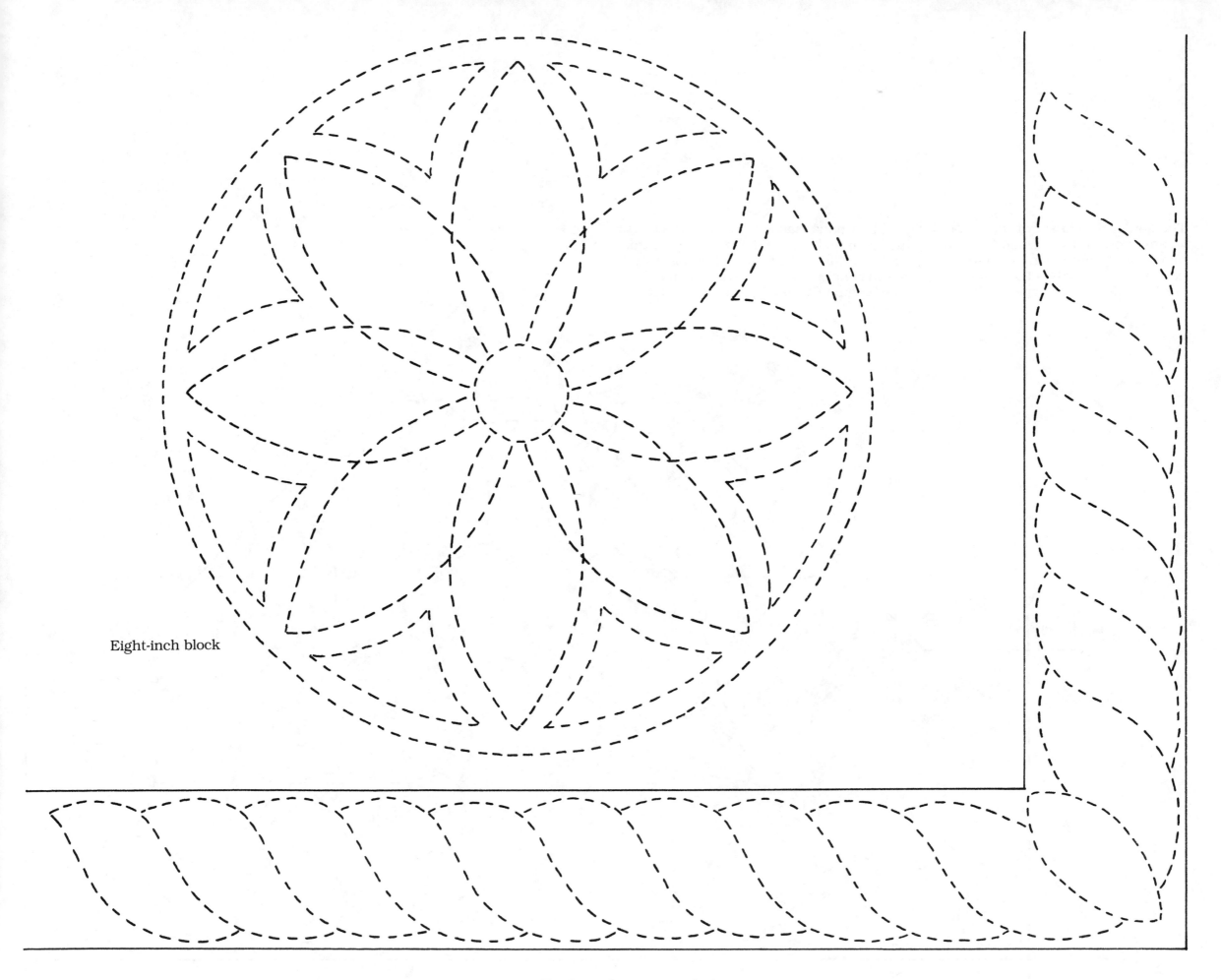

Eight-inch block

Border or lattice strip design

The border design shown here was designed by Donna Hanson Eines of Edmonds, Washington, and quilted on the Double Nine Patch quilt featured on the cover of this book. The combination of workmanship and beautiful quilting won first place and best-of-show awards at the Island County Fair in Langley, Washington and a first place and best-of-category award at the Western Washington Fair in Puyallup, Washington.

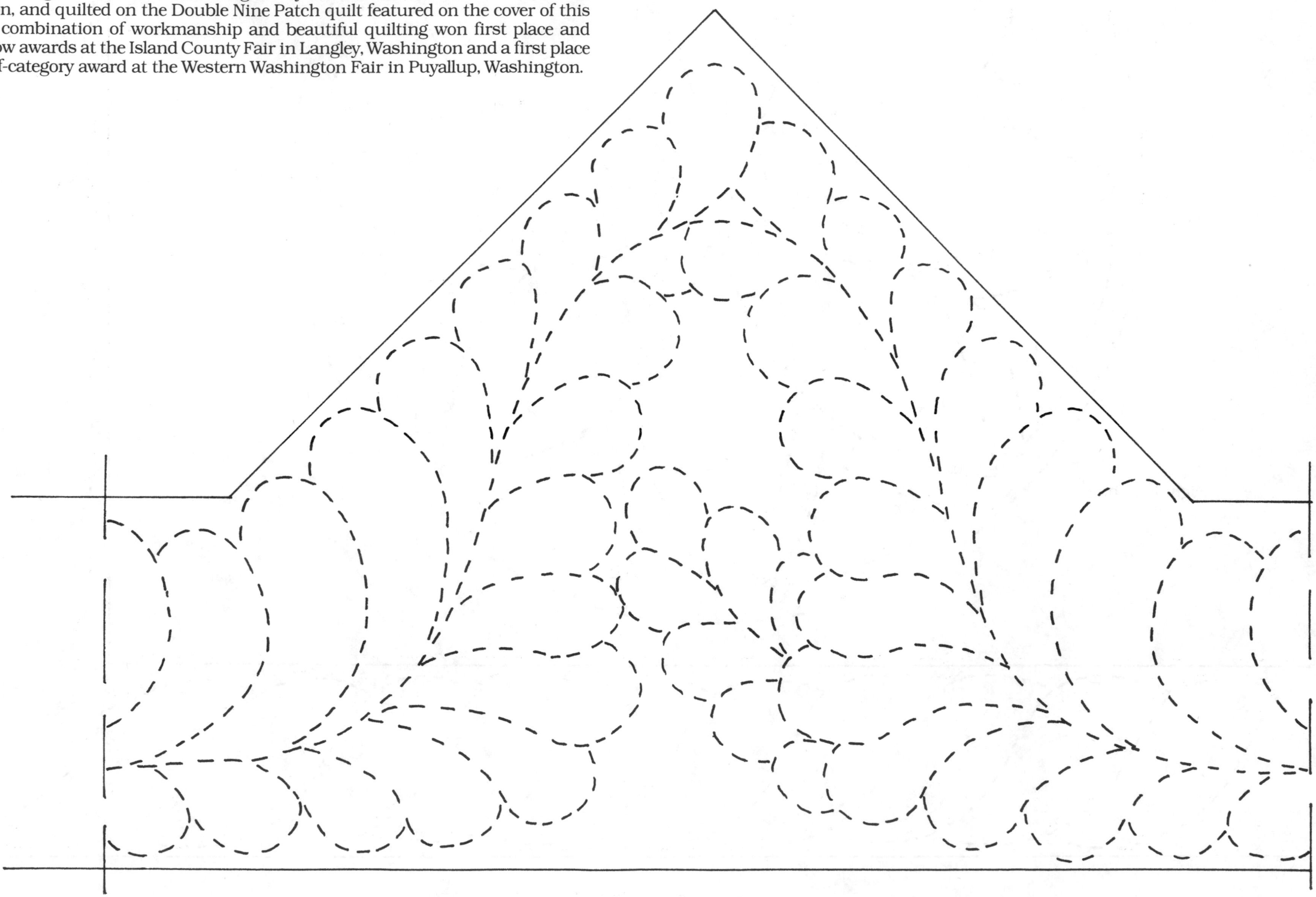

Trace corner design as shown above for left side of corner and flip over for right side of corner.

11

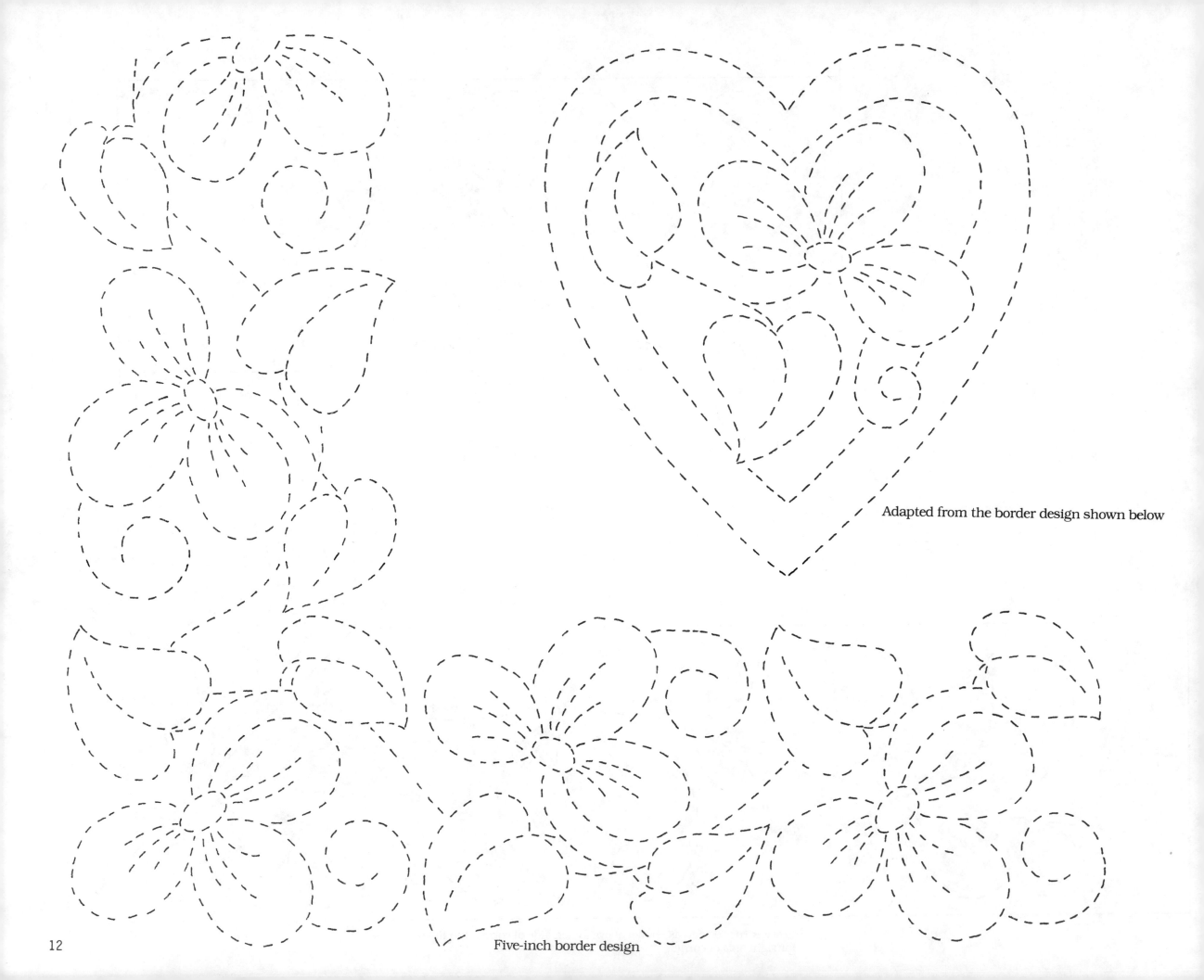

Adapted from the border design shown below

12

Five-inch border design

This eight-inch design was adapted from the border design on the preceding page

Repeat for border design

Six-inch block

The design shown above and the corner design on the preceding
page were adapted from an antique quilting stencil.

Two-inch border or lattice strip     15

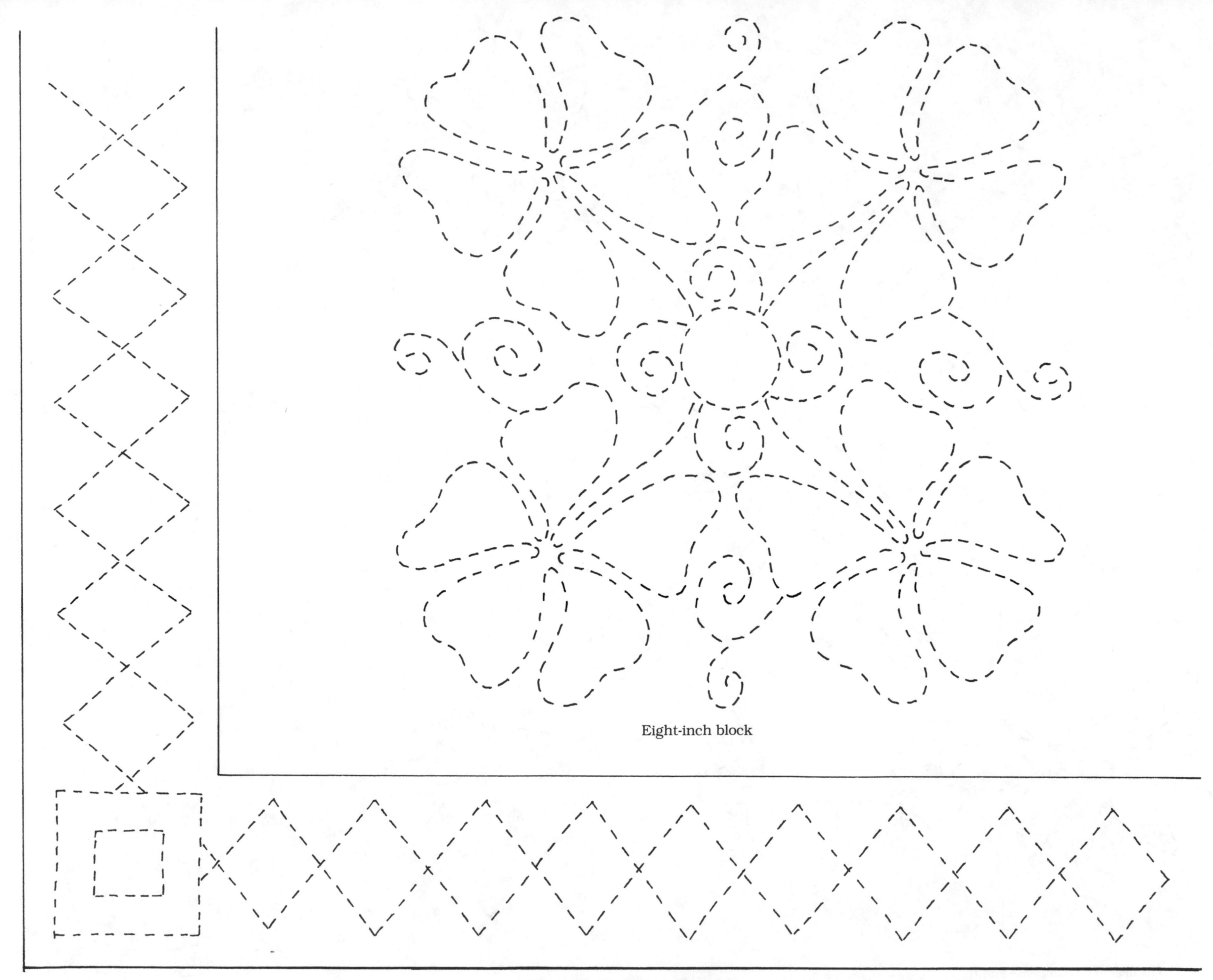

Eight-inch block

Two-inch border or lattice strip

Five-inch block

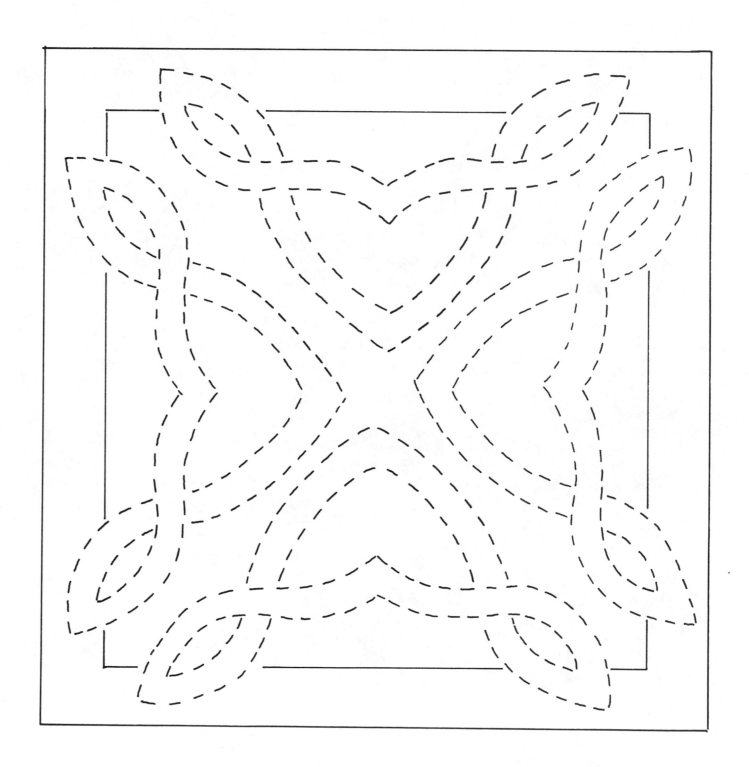

Seven-inch block

Four-inch border

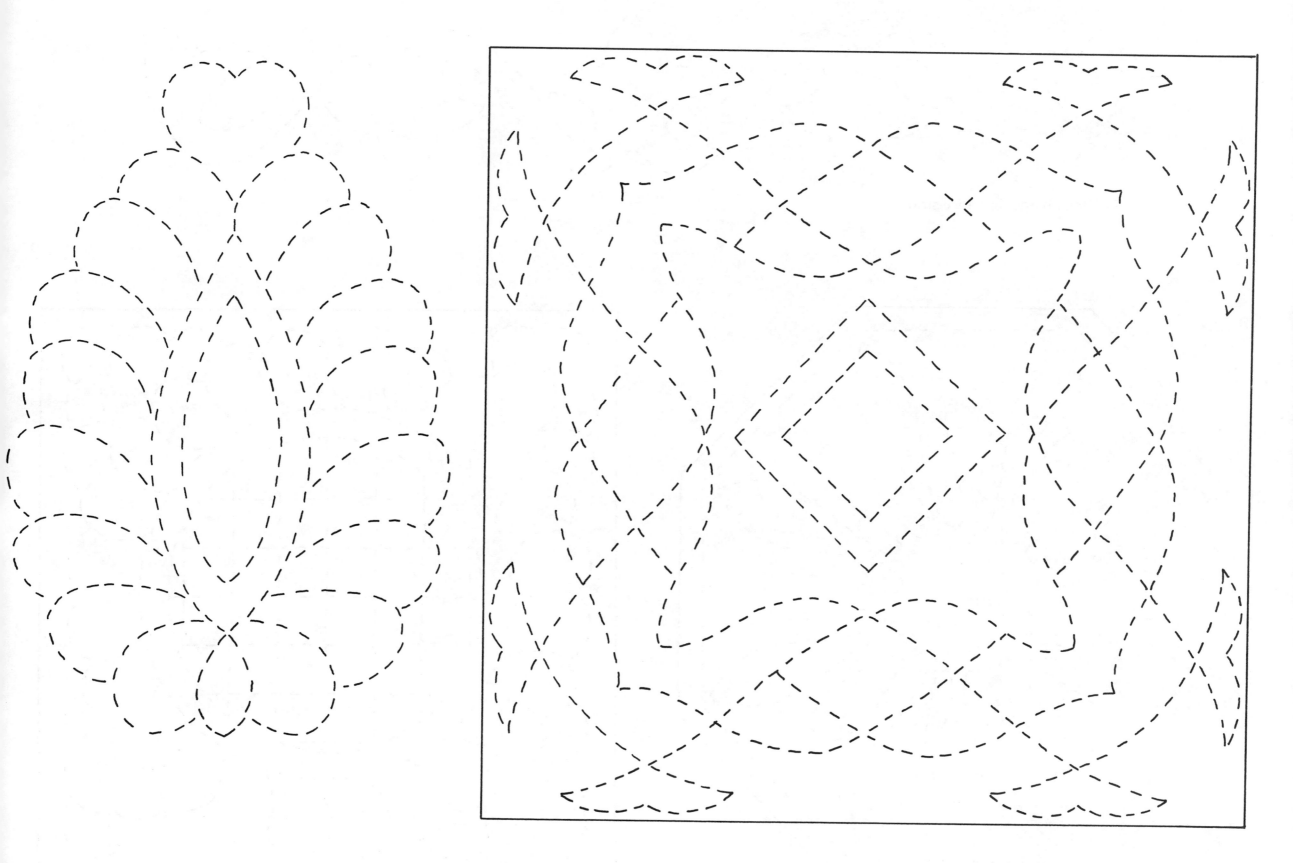

Eight-inch block

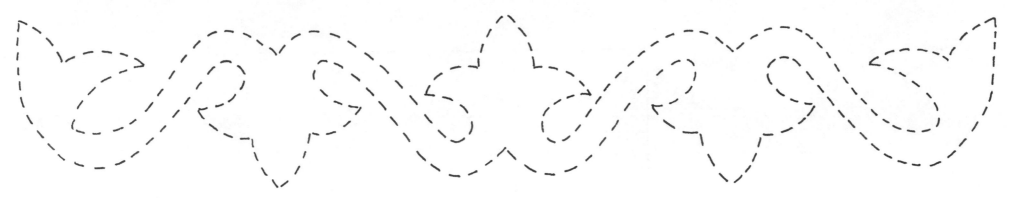

Two-inch border or lattice strip

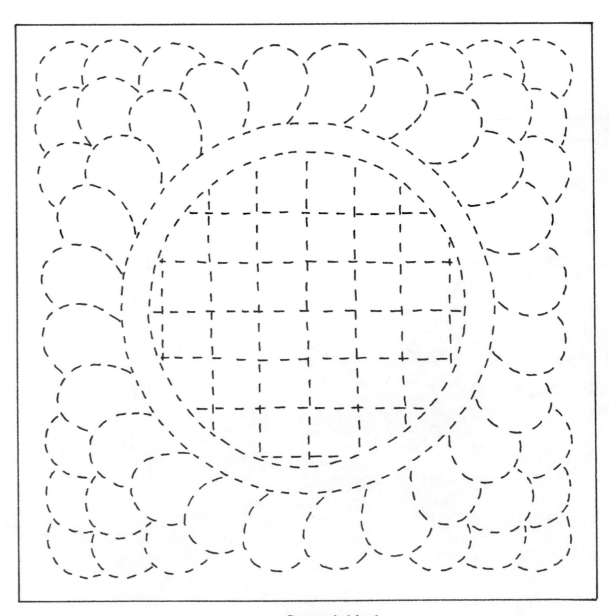

Six-inch block

This is the center section from the eleven-inch block on the following Page.

Eleven-inch block

Ten-inch block

Two-inch border

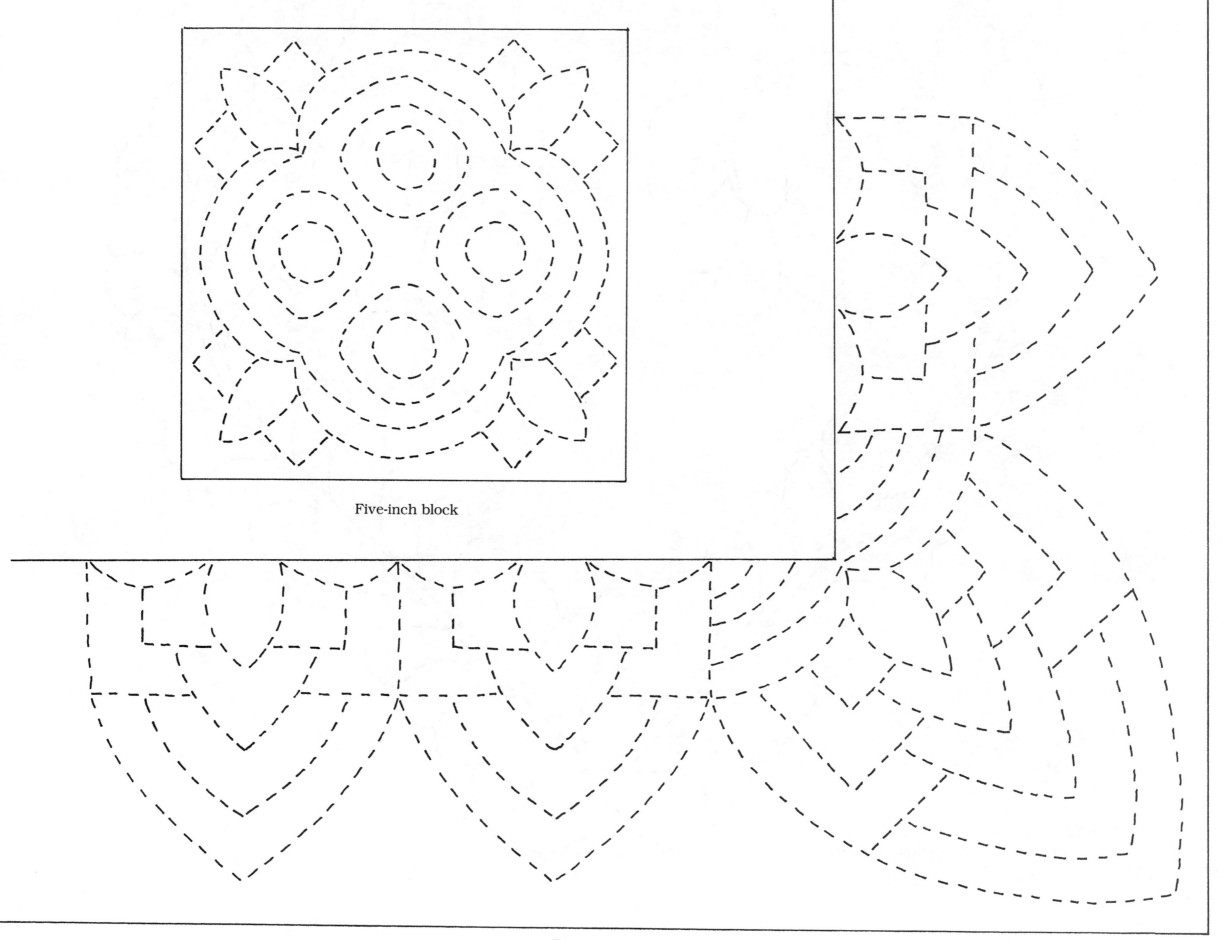

Five-inch block

Four-inch border

Plain blocks alternated with pieced blocks leave
perfect areas for beautiful quilting designs.

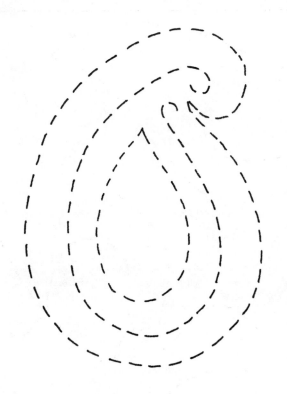

One fourth of an eighteen-inch block

Four-inch block

Four-inch block

Use one fourth of this eight-inch design for a small triangle shaped block or divide the design in half diagonally for a large triangle shaped block.

26

Repeat for a five-inch border
or use alone as a block design.

Border design

Elaborate quilting may be used in areas of the quilt not taken up with pieced or appliqued patterns.

One fourth of a twelve-inch block

Two-inch border or lattice strip

One fourth of a twelve-inch block

Eight-inch block

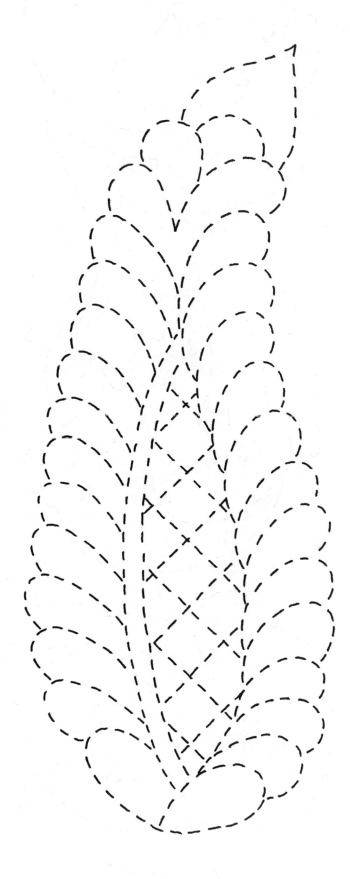

This design was adapted from the border shown below.

Six-inch block

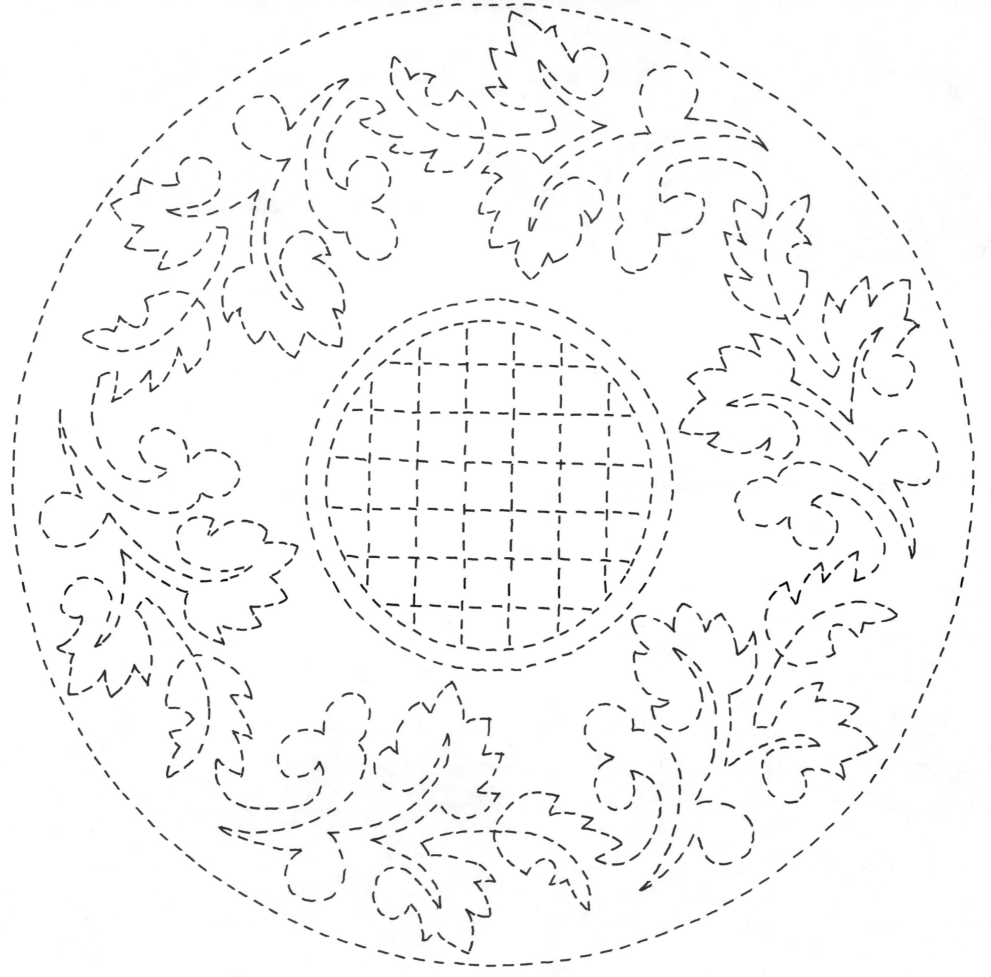

This ten-inch block was adapted from the border design on page thirty-two.

This two-inch border puffs up nicely when quilted.

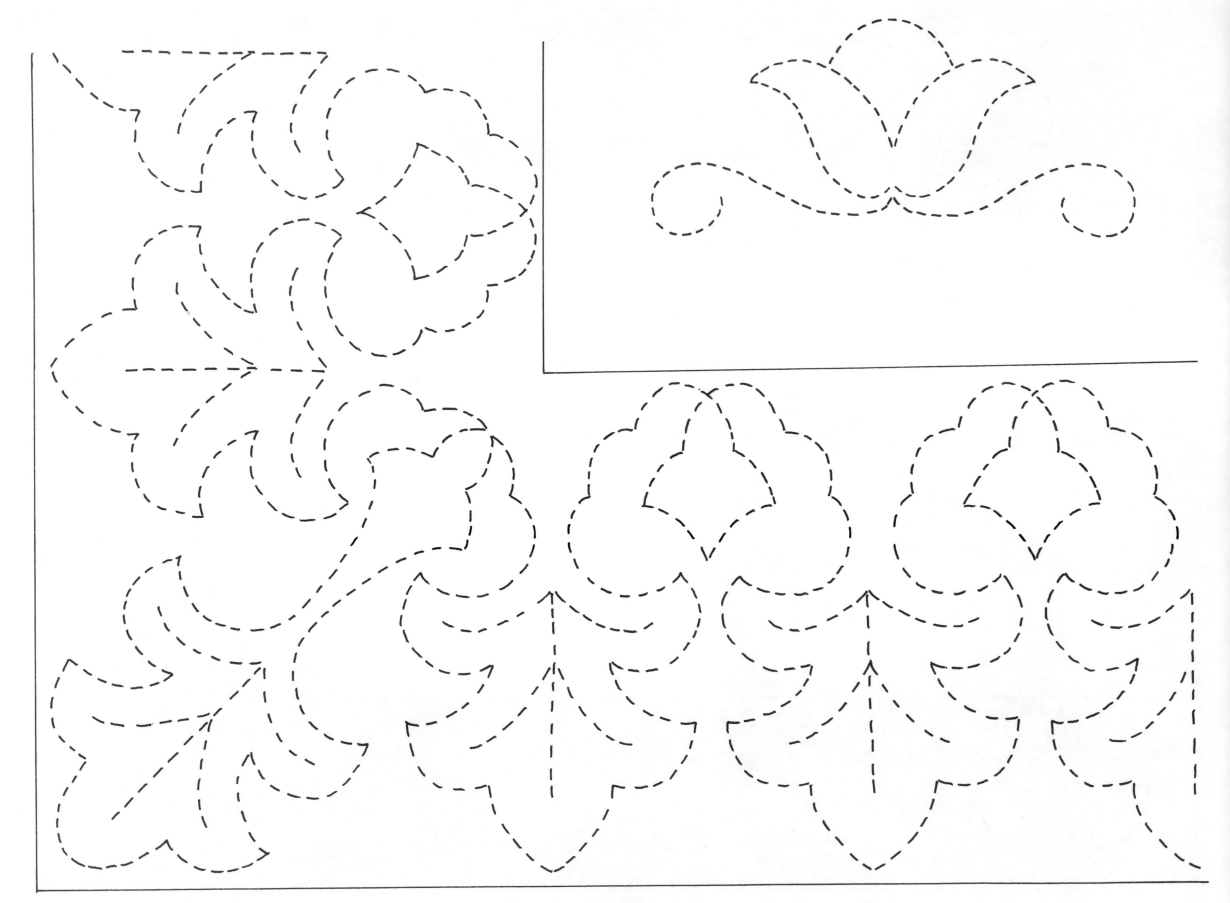

Border design

This design would be a good choice for alternating plain blocks.

Repeat for a lattice or border design

Elaborate quilting may be used in areas of the quilt not taken up with pieced or appliqued patterns.

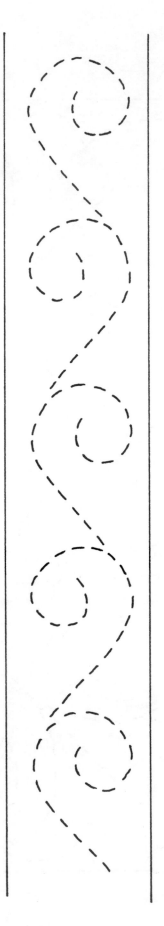

Border or lattice strip design

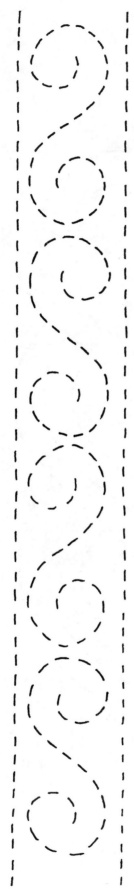

Lattice or border design

One fourth of an eighteen-inch block.

Eight-inch block

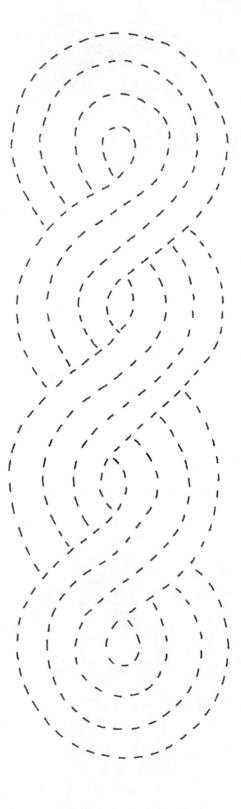

Repeat for a border design.

Repeat for a border design.

Three-inch border

One fourth of an eighteen-inch blcok

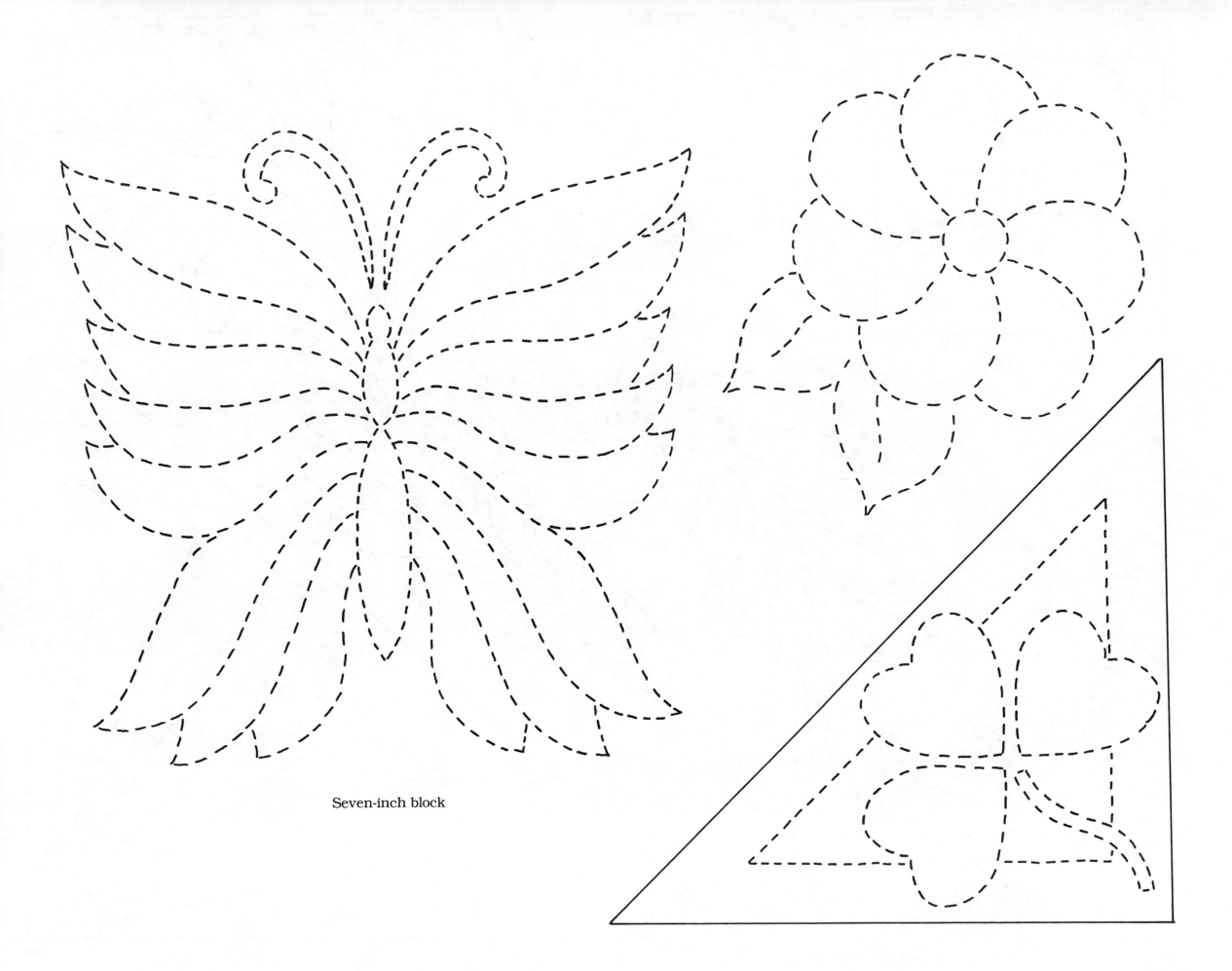

Seven-inch block

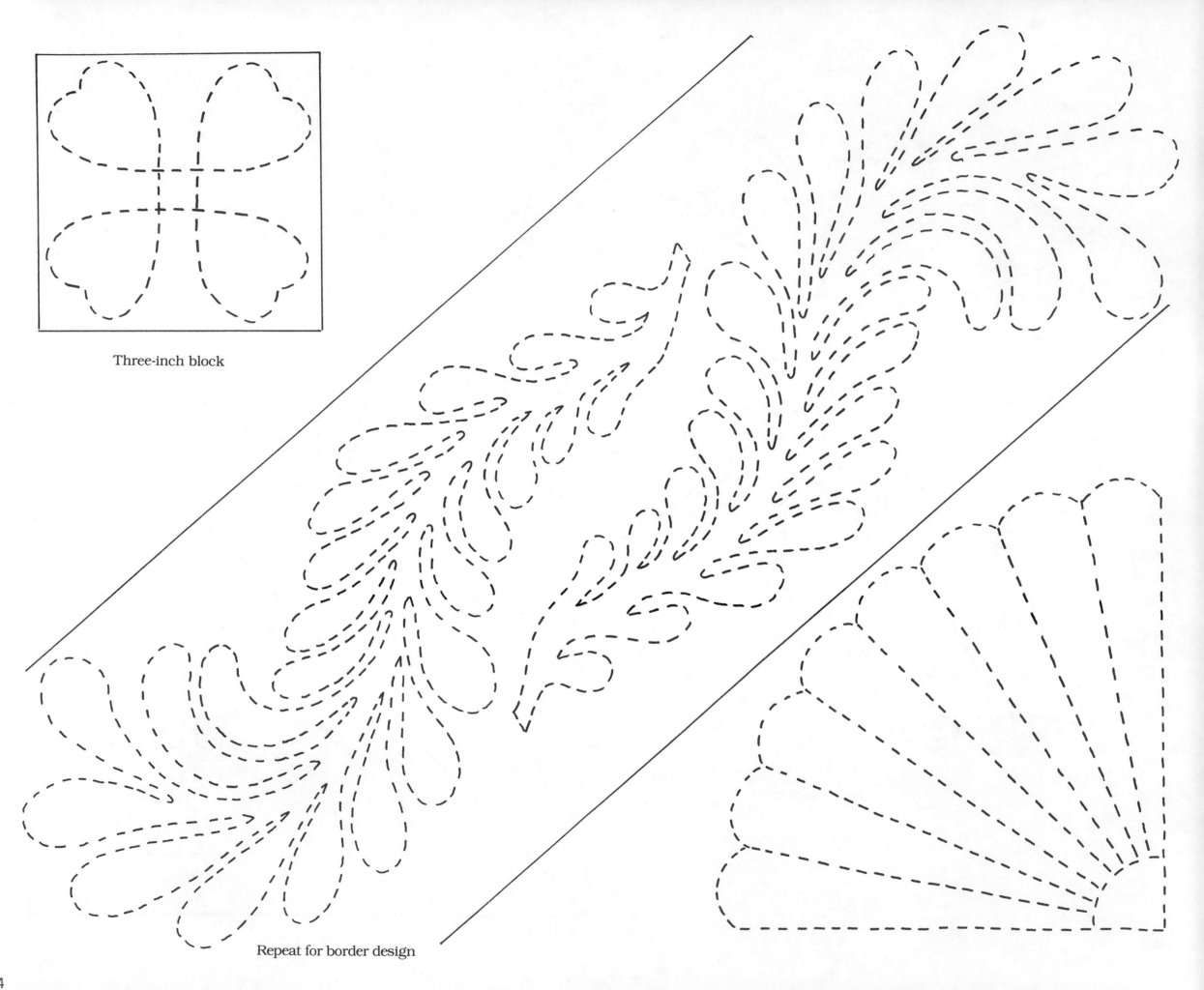

Three-inch block

Repeat for border design

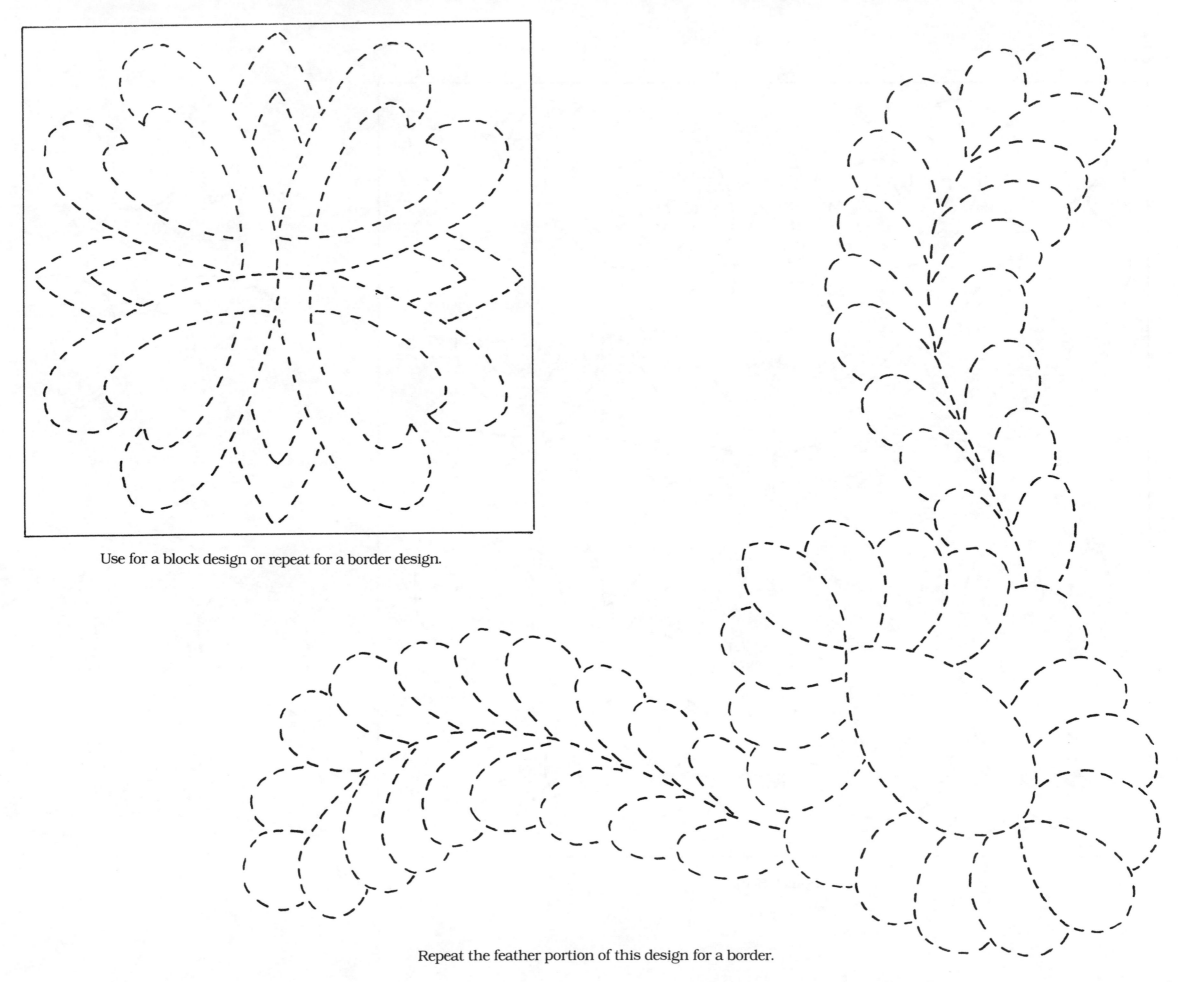

Use for a block design or repeat for a border design.

Repeat the feather portion of this design for a border.

Eight-inch block

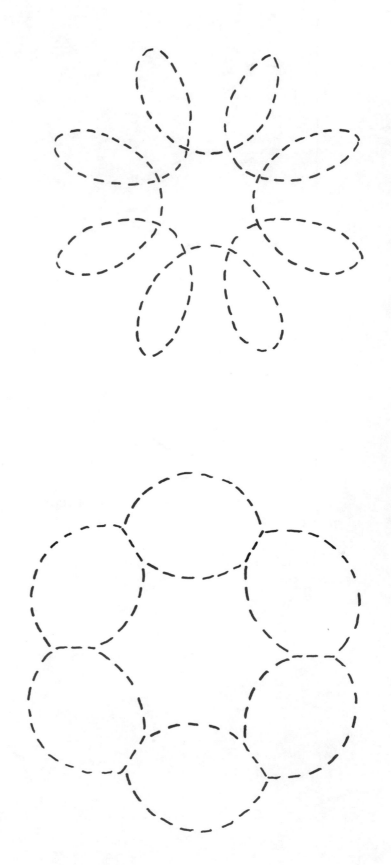

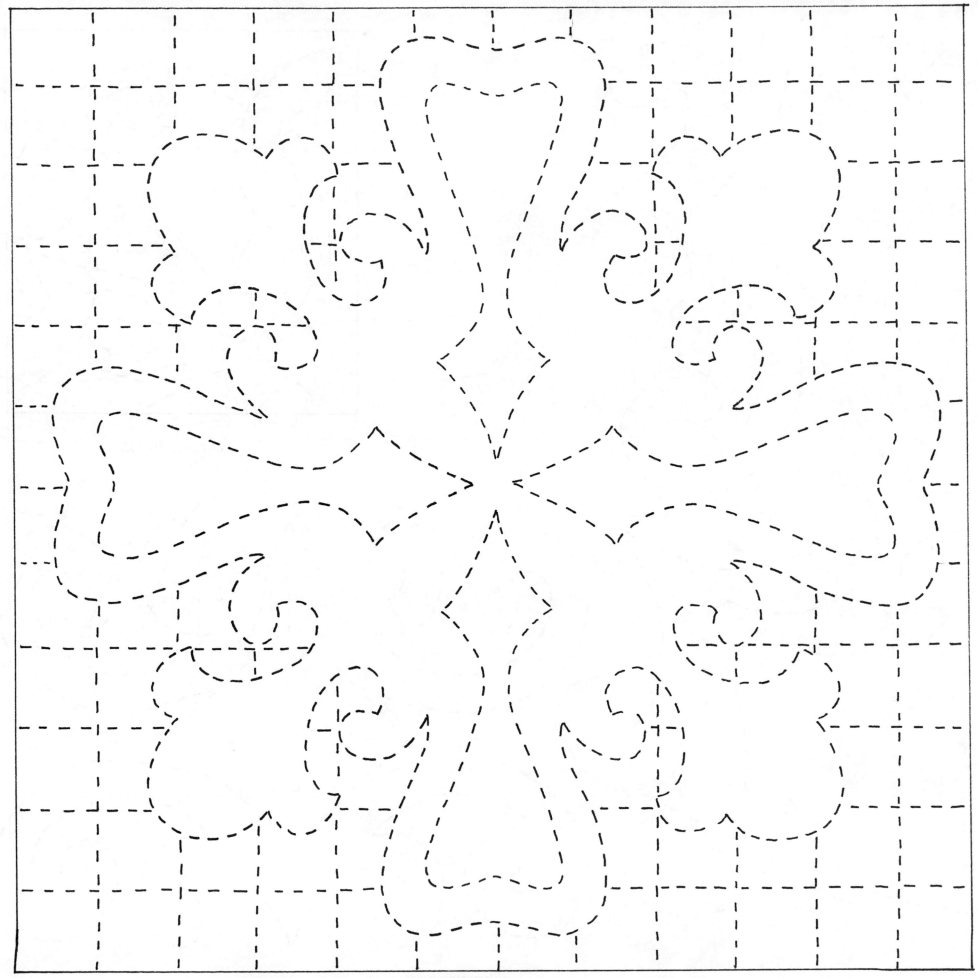

Many of the designs in this book can be made larger by surrounding
them with a filler design of diamonds or diagonal lines.

Four-inch block

Five-inch border

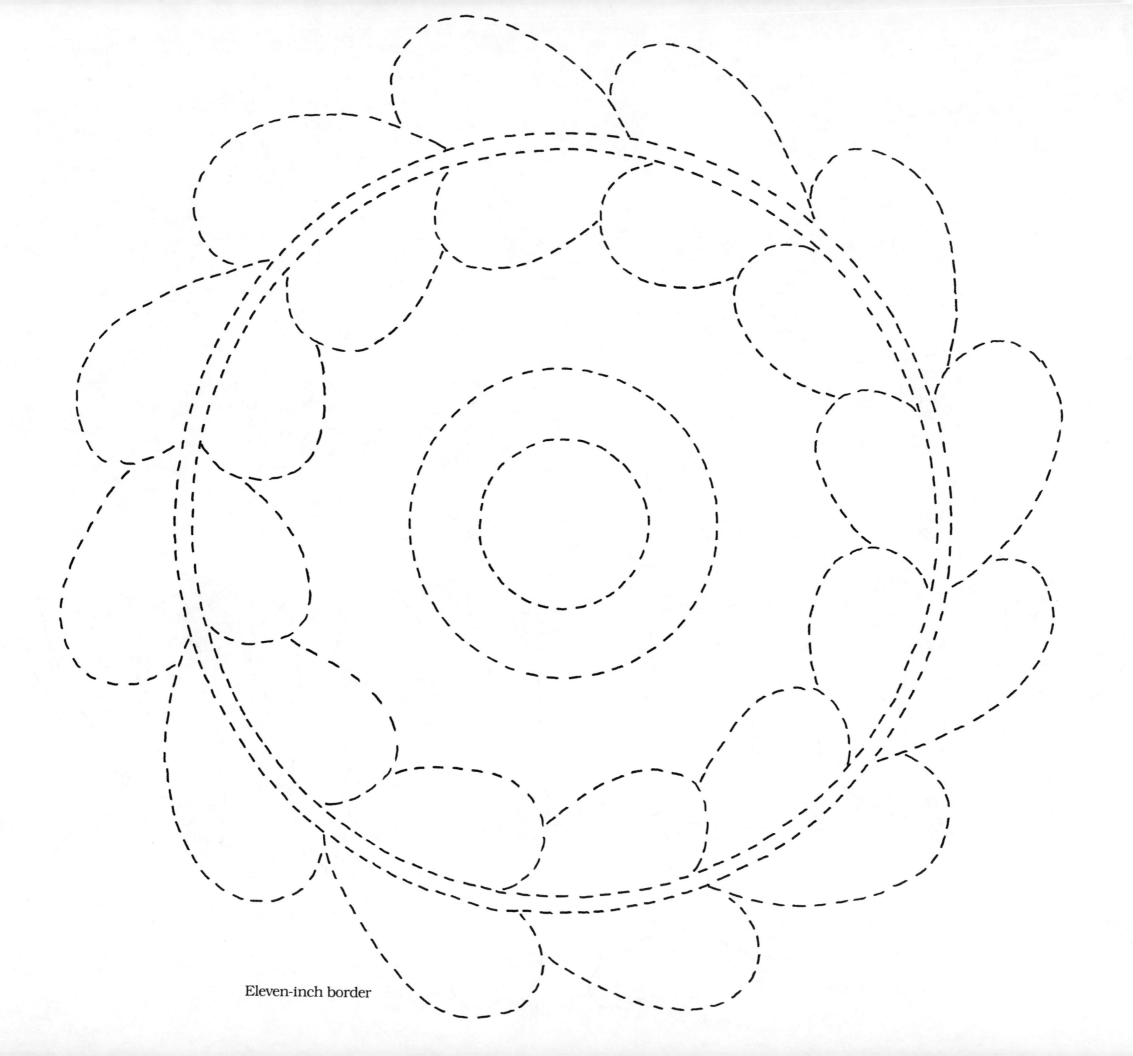

Eleven-inch border

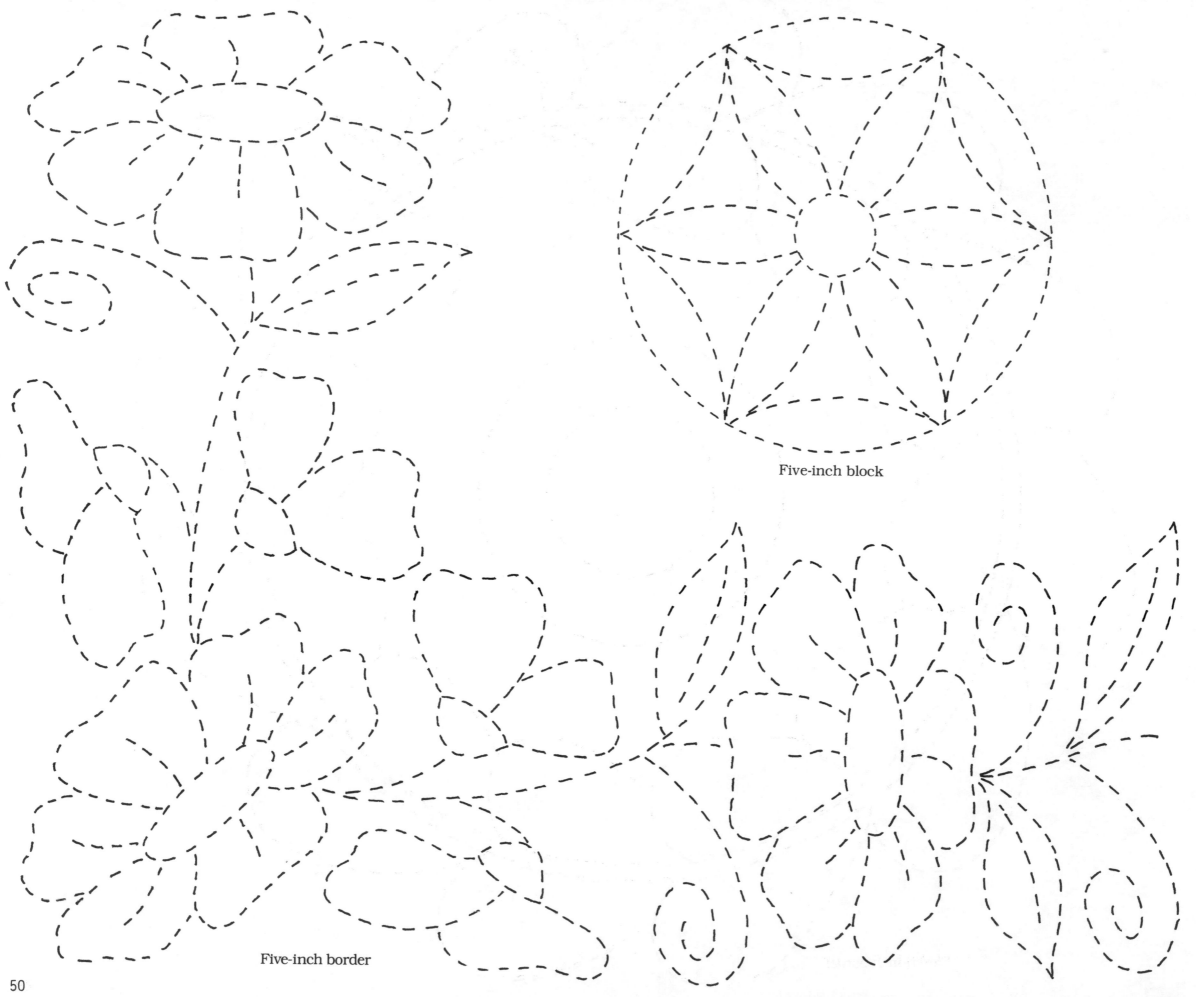

Five-inch block

Five-inch border

The nine-inch block shown here was adapted from the border design on page fifty.

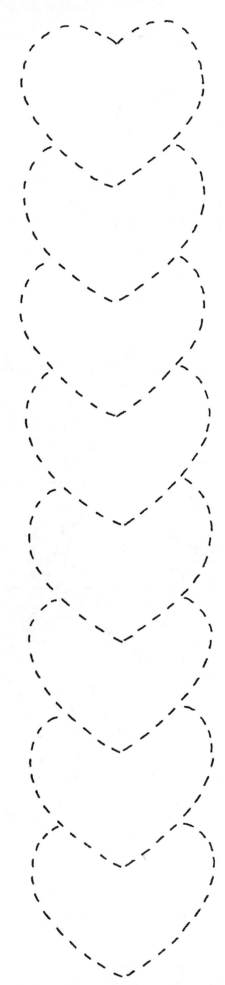

Two-inch border or lattice strip design 51

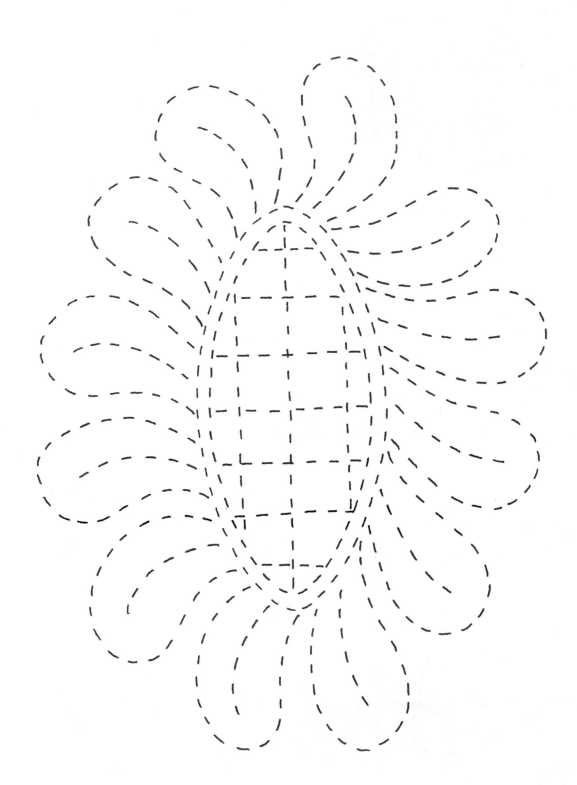

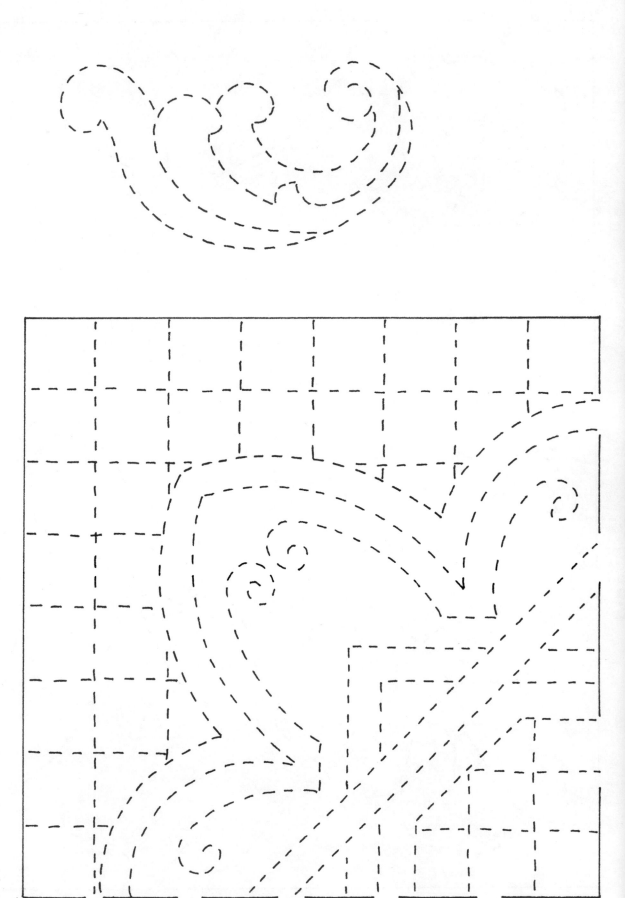

One fourth of a twelve-inch block

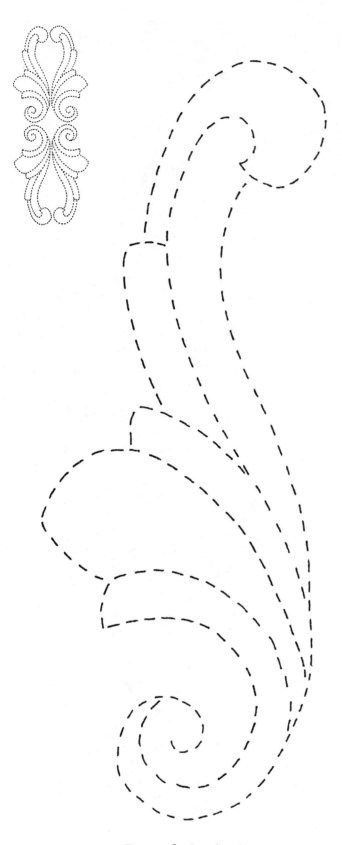

Repeat for border design

Eight-inch blcok

Use the designs shown here for the Double Wedding Ring pattern.

Use this design alone or repeat for a border.

Eight-inch block